SALES STRATEGIES

MW01245573

HOW I SOLD MORE BUSINESS IN ONE WEEK THAN ANY OTHER WEEK IN MY 45-YEAR SALES CAREER

BERNIE GURSTEIN

outskirts
press

Foreword

Being asked to write the foreword of a book written by one of your sales mentors is a lot like winning an award. Or perhaps, more appropriately, like making a sale.

I began selling advertising in the mid 1980s, but it was in October 1987 that my career commenced. That was when I began selling advertising for *ICS Cleaning Specialist Magazine*, and it was not long after that when I met Bernie Gurstein.

Bernie was the owner of a cleaning equipment manufacturing company and a customer of ICS. At the time, U.S. Products (Bernie's company) was not my account. However, that never kept me from building a relationship with our customers, whether they were my accounts or not. Especially since, at this time, I was typically the only person (sales or editorial) representing us at the multiple national and regional trade shows around the country.

Likewise, Bernie was everywhere, and it became common for us to have breakfast or just chat for a while off the floor. These talks invariably were about sales, and Bernie shared many success stories, not to brag but rather to impart his wisdom on a young salesman.

Over the years, I had taken over this account and

worked with Bernie on his advertising programs; however, our friendship transcended our business relationship. I regarded Bernie as a mentor who truly cared about my success and the success of others, and it was indeed this empathy and skill that was a secret to his sales success.

In *Sales Strategies: How I Sold More Business in One Week Than in Any Other Week in My 45-Year Career*, Bernie shares fail-proof strategies to close nearly every presentation.

Enjoy his stories, learn his easy strategies, and *succeed*!

—*Evan Kesslar*
Director of Integrated Media Sales, ALM Media
Former Publisher, ICS Cleaning Specialist Magazine

Table of Contents

Prologue I

Who Is This Bernie Gurstein Anyway? 3

Bernie, Why Did You Write This Book? 10

So, Bernie, How Do You
Actually Accomplish This? 13

This Salesman Was Thinking Out of the Box. 17

"It's an Ongoing Problem...
We can't do anything with it."… 18

Now to the Main Event 21

Sales Call—Experience #1 23

Sales Call—Experience #2 26

Sales Call—Experience #3 29

Sales Call—Experience #4 31

Sales Call—Experience #5 34

Sales Call—Experience #6 36

PMA 38

The 80/20 Rule 38

What Is a Salesperson Anyway? 39

Are You Just a Good Conversationalist? 40

"And the Blue Fairy Came Down..." 41

This Salesman Was Dead in the Water 43

Again, It's Simple: No Close, No Sale! 47

Six Out of Six Calls 48

Making the Close— Hard or Soft 50

My Ten-Word Close Resulted in a $2,000 Sale 52

Show Note: My Wife's Suggestion
Turned into a Major Source of Business 54

As Elmer Wheeler, Noted Author, Says, ... 56

There's the Logical Reason for Not Buying 62

How Your Company Name
Can Greatly Enhance Your Profit Margin 63

What Is a Unit? Whatever You Want It to Be! 66

The Only Caveat Is
It's a 3 a.m. Sales Call... 68

"Bob, You Just Can't Keep Coming in
Every Weekend—Make a Decision!" 70

"Why Did You Hurt That Nice Young Man?" 73

How NOT to Get In to Nine Out of Ten Calls 74

Now, How to GET IN to Nine Out of Ten Calls .. 76

Impressive Demo Products 78

Selling Quality Over Price 81

The Most Unforgettable,
Exasperating, Frustrating, ... 86

The Salesman Grabbed Him
and Threatened Him 90

My Magic "Abracadabra" Sale 95

The "Shit and Piss" Sale 97

"You Are the Toughest Lady Executive
Housekeeper That I Have Ever Called On!" 99

Money Makes the World Go Around. .. .. .100

My Negative Sales Close
Ended Up To Be a Positive. 101

The Start of My Career—Selling "Babee Tenda". . 103

Babee Tenda Sale #1—The Hot Button 104

Babee Tenda Sale #2—One of My
More Stressful Sales 106

We Really Did Close
Six Out of Six Sales Calls! 108

In Closing, Here Are Two
Fantastic Books That I Recommend Highly. 113

Prologue

This book teaches you lessons in salesmanship. As you walk through each call with me, you will learn about introductions, presentations, and demonstrations. You will also discover how to master *the most important skill of all, the "nemesis" of most salespeople; the close.*

Although this is a sales book, it is entertainingly presented as a series of short stories. You will find intrigue, suspense, anxiety, and even some humor as you experience these interesting sales calls with me. Even though this book is slanted toward the sanitary/ janitorial industry, the lessons—and especially the "close" information—can be applied to any industry. These lessons, hints, and tips can be integrated into your sales techniques to ensure your success. Even if you pick up just one or two ideas, that can make the book worth your time and money.

Who Is This
Bernie Gurstein Anyway?

My name is Bernie Gurstein. I am a professional salesman who became the creator and owner of three separate successful businesses. We started in our garage like so many entrepreneurs have, going for the American dream. Our first company was U.S. Research & Chemical located in Woodland Hills, California. *(Further on in the book, you'll learn how our company name alone was responsible for thousands of dollars of additional business.)* We sold sanitary/janitorial supplies, carpet cleaning and upholstery/drapery cleaning machines, and chemical solutions. We also offered repairs, rentals, etc.

Our second business, a maintenance service, was run under our U.S. Research & Chemical name. Our third business was born after several profitable years and a bout with burnout. Through the years, working with and selling janitorial equipment, I began to see ways in which these items were lacking, and I had ideas on how to improve them. I decided I wanted to move into the actual manufacturing of the equipment that we sold at U.S. Research & Chemical. The result was the creation of U.S. Products, Inc. I'm sure many of you readers are familiar with one or both of our company names.

U.S. Products building

U.S. Products production line

At U.S. Products, we designed and manufactured carpet and upholstery cleaning equipment and floor cleaning equipment, as well as tools and accessories that sold worldwide. We were a family operation, focused on creative solutions, quality products, and success. Together with my son, son-in-law, daughter, and wife, we created a company with the most unique equipment in the industry.

Our first breakthrough was high-heat capability for carpet cleaning machines. We didn't invent the heat exchanger, but we were responsible for engineering and designing the first heat exchanger for carpet cleaning equipment. Our machines gave the operator the ability to clean with 200-degree hot water at the spray tip. The heat, along with a high 300 PSI pump, increased efficiency dramatically and the operator could now clean 40 percent to 50 percent more carpet than his or her competition. (It was like having a truck mount in a portable cleaning machine.)

Our second breakthrough came with the introduction of our wet- and dry-cleaning machine. Now the professional cleaner had the ability to wet-clean with heated water or dry-clean with our procedure for safely cleaning with a heated dry-cleaning solution! (This was a patented feature.)

This machine also allowed for dry-cleaning draperies where they hung. There was no fear of shrinkage (a problem with wet cleaning), when cleaning with a solvent. Therefore, there was no need for loaners, so the

High-heat/high PSI carpet cleaning machines and wet/ dry high-heat upholstery/drapery cleaning machine

removal of the drapes was eliminated. Several major hotels purchased the equipment from our distributors for use in-house. *In the meantime, the professional cleaner was earning $100 to $200 an hour dry-cleaning draperies and fine upholstery!*

We were running full-page color ads every month informing the trade of our machines' advantages. Our reputation grew rapidly. Other companies started copying our heat exchanger, but our equipment was among the highest-quality products in the industry, and we retained a strong edge over our competition. Almost all of our equipment had patented features, and eventually we had a total of fifteen patents. The experts say, "Think out of the box," and that's what we did. Our novel ideas and great success were the result.

Another innovation of ours was a superior shampoo tank. (Shampoo tanks hold the cleaning solution when scrubbing carpets or floors.) This tank was unique because we were the only manufacturer that offered it in colors to match the company's color scheme. We also were the only manufacturer to offer a lifetime warranty.

Initially, we began selling one to two dozen tanks a month. Then we decided to advertise it internationally in the key trade magazines, which our competition

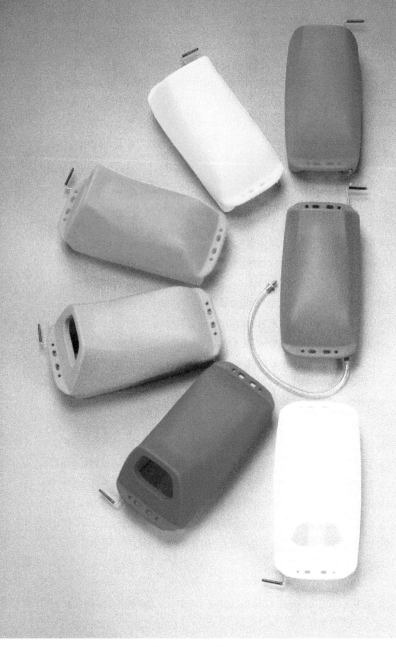

Multi-colored shampoo tanks

was not doing. Shortly afterward, we started receiving orders from all over the world. So, we took a product that you would normally classify as a basic commodity and transformed it into a first-class, in-demand, major addition to our line. *When we sold our company several years later, we were selling an amazing 1,200 to 1,300 shampoo tanks per month!*

Bernie, Why Did You Write This Book?

And who can benefit from it?

My wife wanted me to write this book many years ago. She felt that my sales strategies and my many interesting success stories would be very helpful to other salespeople. Although she is gone now, I'm finally finding the motivation to do it.

As I said in the prologue, this book is primarily aimed at the sanitary/janitorial supply industry, but **you can apply these ideas and sales techniques to any industry or product.** The sanitary supply salesperson must do demonstrations of his or her products from time to time, just as the office equipment salesperson does for his or her equipment—copiers, scanners, computers, etc. No matter what business you are in, a good professional demonstration with a strong close usually turns into a sale.

It is also a tremendous advantage not only to know your product inside out, but to **know your competition's product, as well.** I cannot stress this enough. *Without knowledge of your competition's product, the chances of a sale can go down significantly!* Several times in my career, knowledge of my competition's product literally saved the day!

Remember to stay opportunity conscious; when you see or hear about a good idea, write it down. You may be able to apply one of those ideas to your own business or to your sales presentation. To this day, I write down good ideas. You never know who in your family or who of your friends can benefit from them.

I am not selling hype here. I have not discovered the mystic secrets on how to make you a millionaire. In reality, what I discovered, or rediscovered, is a basic sales concept that I have used in the past and probably you have, too. The difference is, in one five-day training session with my trainee (description to follow), we learned how successful this basic sales technique really is and how to apply it! We focused and zeroed in on it.

I stated on the cover of this book, *I did more business in one week than I did in any other week in my entire forty-five-year sales career!* If you have a hard time believing that, my next statement is going to be even harder to believe.

The average good professional salesperson will close one sale out of every three calls. **We sold six out of seven customers! That's an 85 percent closing ratio!** If I stated that on the cover, you probably would have thought this guy is a dreamer or a scammer, making unbelievable statements to sell his book. You'll see the light as you read further. A closing ratio of 85 percent is even more important to a salesperson than how much business he or she writes, although if he or she can actually close that high of a percentage, then the business will automatically be there.

In sales, it's easy to make ten calls before you locate that one qualified prospect. So, what would happen if you could eliminate all of those calls and only call on that qualified prospect *every time*? I'll tell you exactly what would happen: you would accomplish an 85 percent closing ratio as my trainee and I did. If not 85 percent, certainly 60 percent or 70 percent. No matter, *this is unheard of and a salesperson's dream!*

So, Bernie, How Do You Actually Accomplish This?

As I thought back over my years in sales, I realized that most of my successes were the result of solving a prospect's problem, be it a wood floor that needed refinishing, or carpet, upholstery, or drapes that could not be cleaned; there was always something. You just have to stay alert and be aware of the problems all around you.

Here is a <u>prime example:</u> I had an appointment to see my attorney in this large office building. As I entered, I observed a maintenance man shampooing/scrubbing the carpet with a floor machine, a shampoo brush, and a shampoo tank full of cleaning solution. Using this system is okay for very dirty carpet and should be followed up with a carpet extractor to suck out the dirty solution. *If you just continue to shampoo the carpet without extracting the solution, after months or years, the dirty solution absorbed by the carpet starts to surface and become visible.*

This is exactly what I was witnessing here. This was a great prospect for our carpet extractor. I located the executive housekeeper and was prepared to enlighten her on the carpet problem. She cut me off and said, "We really can't get this carpet clean anymore.

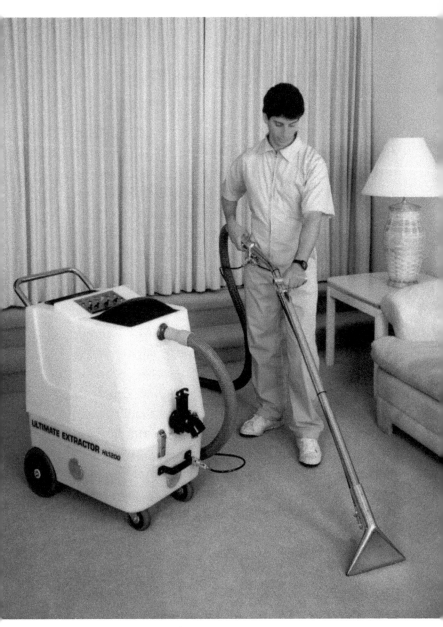

Carpet extractor in use

The owners are going to replace the carpet in the entire building."

"Wow," I said, *"you are talking several thousands of dollars!* I have been in this business for years and have the expertise to show you how to clean this carpet and not have to replace it. If we can see the owners, I can explain how we can accomplish this."

She was all for this solution and called their office. They were in, and we were on our way. In the office, I explained the condition of the carpet and how it happened. They were, of course, very interested. At this stage, I concluded with "We can still save the carpet and eliminate having to replace it. I can return tomorrow with our high-tech cleaning extractor and do a test. Let me know what time works for you to return and do the demonstration." The next day we cordoned off a ten-foot square section of carpet to clean.

There was so much detergent left in the carpet that I planned to clean with just hot water and a defoamer (to kill the foam from the leftover detergent). The procedure was lengthy, removing months or years of old dirt and detergent. Finally, the extractor did what it was designed for and the carpet really did look like new.

I explained what I was doing to the executive house-keeper and suggested that they order two machines to handle all the carpet in the building. After all, they were saving thousands of dollars. It was a no-contest sale, which came to approximately $4,000. This sale was only possible because of my mindset and constant awareness of problems. This could be you, too!

This Salesman Was Thinking Out of the Box

At his wits end, a salesman sent this note to a very desirable prospect: *"I have been trying to get an appointment to speak to you without any success. I was able to speak to God today; why can't I speak to you?"* Needless to say, he got his appointment. This was very clever, and I wish that I could take credit for it, but it's not my story. This story has been in my head for years and I just wanted to pass it on.

"It's an Ongoing Problem...

We can't do anything with it."

I sold two of my key accounts by solving their problems. The first was a large well-known chain of ten gyms in the Los Angeles area. I ended up with the entire account. Here's how it happened: When I made my initial call on one of the gyms, the vinyl floor glared at me. It was a mess! The manager told me, "It's an ongoing problem. We can't do anything with it." He said many salesmen had tried their products and failed. I had the expertise to know exactly why and how it failed and offered to solve his problem.

Demonstration, Demonstration, Demonstration

I convinced him to let me try to restore the floor. I knew it was not the product but the maintenance of the floor that was the problem. I met with his maintenance man, and we stripped the floor together. Then we sealed it and applied three finish coats. The floor looked fantastic, and the manager was thrilled.

I explained to him that the problem was that his maintenance man had too many duties and was not able to give the floor the attention it needed. I also told him the floor was going to look like we hadn't touched it by the end of the week. However, if he would turn the

*Using proper tools, product and technique
to create high-shine floors*

gym over to our maintenance crew, the floor would look fantastic every single day.

As predicted, the floor was a wreck by the end of the week. As a result, we got the account, and that's how we got started in the maintenance business. After the word got out to the other gyms, we eventually ended up with all of their gyms. This became our largest and most profitable account.

The second key account was a children's camp in Agoura, California. The wood floor in their auditorium was a disaster, and they had a major event scheduled. I offered to work with their maintenance man and re-finish their floor. Besides getting the chance to show them what we could do for their floor, I was able to write a nice order for the products necessary to do the job.

The floor was completely restored, and they were very pleased. The owner's wife was so appreciative, she gave me the gift of a leather wallet as a thank-you. After seeing the results, they became one of my bet-ter key accounts.

Now to the Main Event

My fantastic sales week

After U.S. Research & Chemical became very successful, we decided to dabble in franchises. The first phase
of training the franchisee was customer care and sales
in our store. The second phase was training in how to
make cold calls in the field.

This new franchisee had done the in-store training, and
it was now time to take him out in the field for cold
call training. This put me under some pressure since
he had spent good money to purchase our franchise,
and of course, I wanted him to be successful. I needed
to make sure our cold call sales brought results.

This caused me to look back on how I had created my own success as a salesman. I remembered
how I sold my two biggest/key accounts (mentioned
earlier) and came up with the sales plan to simply
look for problems that needed solving. This would
eliminate having to make call after call. *My main
concern was would we find enough businesses
with problems to follow through with our sales
plan? It ended up not being a concern at all.* Even
though it took some additional time locating those
qualified prospects, our time was well-spent and
very productive. After all, we weren't wasting time

calling on unqualified prospects as we soon proved in the real world.

My trainee was from the Palm Desert/Palm Springs area in California, so that is where we started our venture or, in this case, our "learning adventure." Driving time was approximately four hours from my business location in the San Fernando Valley, California, to where I would be working with my trainee; therefore, we did not have that much time in the field—approximately four hours. One or two sales a day was our goal. All we did was literally drive through the business district looking for unresolved issues. It materialized into a salesman's dream!

Here is a breakdown of our sales calls. I would like to explain here that because of possible legal issues—especially with the major accounts—I am not mentioning any of the sales customers by name.

Sales Call—Experience #1

"I know we have a problem.
Can you help me?"

A relatively new major chain hotel that had been open for approximately one year inspired our first call. What we saw was a walkway extending from the parking lot entrance to the hotel. The walkway was covered by a red awning, approximately fifty to seventy-five feet long. The awning had faded at least 50 percent due to the sun and presented a poor appearance for anyone entering the hotel. We surmised that although this was a major chain hotel, it was probably too new to realize a profit yet, and they were reluctant to spend what would most likely be thousands of dollars to replace it.

We had a product not unlike Armor All, and we decided to do a test patch on the awning and see if we could effectively deepen the red dye and hopefully improve the appearance. Amazingly, the color turned out at least 50 percent better, and the effect was evident. The awning no longer appeared faded.

I got on the phone and located the executive responsible for the awning. I told him that I was aware of the problem with it, that we had done a test patch in an inconspicuous area, and that the results were dramatic.

The usual response for trying to get an appointment with a key person is excuses, put-offs, and sometimes cancellation of your appointment. However, this was a completely different situation: *we had the solution to a problem that could save thousands of dollars!*

We had guessed right. We had stumbled across a problem that perplexed them. We got the response that every salesperson desires: **"I know we have a problem with that awning. Can you help me?"** I thought, "Are you kidding?" When is the last time any one of us had a response like that? "Oh yes, you bet I can help you!" I reiterated that the proof was in our test patch and asked if he could come out and inspect it. Again, we were elated when he said, *"I'll be out in ten minutes!"*

This individual was experienced, and although he was impressed and said it looked great, he wanted to see what it would look like in the morning. He was concerned that it might fade back again. (It possibly could, but not likely.) I said we would be back in the morning, and since he liked what he saw, could we enlarge on the test patch? He gave us his approval and left. We enlarged the test patch from eighteen inches to four square feet. It was now spectacular, which is exactly the effect that we wanted. He had to buy now!

The morning meeting was everything we had anticipated and more. He was very impressed, and we sold him not only the product but also All Purpose Cleaner to prepare and clean the awning, along with long-handled brushes for scrubbing, sponges, towels, sprayers, etc. The coup de grâce was an introduction to the executive housekeeper to whom we ended up selling a shampoo machine promotion. Our sale was just under $3,000, plus, of course, the resulting repeat business.

In analyzing our sale, we simply felt fortunate enough to spot this problem that was solvable with a key product. At that stage, we were just beginning to see the big picture.

Sales Call—Experience #2

The owner was in shock.
"You ruined my floor!"

Our next call was to a delightful resort featuring cabins on rolling green hills with many trees. We thought that our Speedfoamer promotion (free carpet cleaning machine with purchase of fifty-five gallons of shampoo) would be perfect for maintaining the cabins. However, when we walked into the main building where the lounge and eating area were, I put the shampoo promotion on the back burner. Although these areas were clean and well-maintained, the wood floor in the restaurant was starting to show obvious signs of traffic wear.

This was similar to the awning problem at the hotel. Here was an obvious problem, and we had the solution. This appeared to be a very successful operation. I didn't think that money was a concern. They were simply living with the problem. Nobody had taken responsibility for it.

The owner was available and in a good humor. He invited us into his office and asked what he could do for us. "Actually," I said, "there is something I can do for you!" I asked him to follow me, and we stopped at the wood floor in his restaurant. I complimented him on his first-class operation but said that the condition of his wood floor was distracting from it.

Again, we hit the nail on the head. He was well aware of the problem and had been concerned about it, but he was just not finding the time to handle it. It was easier to procrastinate. I commented that we had all been there, but I was in a position to solve the problem. All he had to do was order the products I recommended and supply a couple of people to be trained and we would supervise the operation. He said, "You have a deal."

We sold him fifteen gallons of our very best moisture-curing urethane at fifty dollars a gallon, sanding screens to surface-sand the floor, applicators, solvent, rags, mop heads, etc.—a very nice sale, indeed.

But that was not the end of it. I noticed his lobby floor was made up of twelve-inch quarry tiles. It appeared that they had been waxing it for years. I could tell by how dark the floor had become. It did not look that bad since the dark wax color was consistent. There were no traffic areas showing. It was simply well overdue for a stripping and recoating. I asked him if I could do a test on a couple of the tiles. He said yes and then went into his office to take a phone call.

Without any exaggeration, the test tiles that I stripped

came out ten shades lighter. It was very impressive. When the owner returned, however, his reaction was shock. He blurted out, "You ruined my floor!" I chuckled and said, "No, this is the original color. This is how it is supposed to look. This floor was in much need of stripping, sealing, and recoating." I told him the floor probably had not been stripped in many years.

After he calmed down, he recognized the situation for what it was. He said, "What do we have to do to get the rest of the floor to look like the test tiles?" I told him I'd write an order for the products that he would need, and when we came back to do the wood floor, I'd go over the procedure for stripping and finishing his tiles with his men. We wrote another order for stripper, sealer, floor finish, and applicators.

Although we had to come back to fulfill our part of the agreement, it was well worth it. That commitment on our part is exactly what secured the sale. The sale now was for approximately $4,000, plus future business.

By the way, the wood floors came out great! However, they had not yet stripped the lobby floors when I last checked in.

Sales Call—Experience #3

An alkaline film reduced the view by 50 percent

One day we stopped for lunch at a golf course restaurant. After lunch, on our way out, I noticed a huge glass window in front of the bar. Through the window was a magnificent view of the golf course. The only problem was that the window was fogged over with an alkaline film that had formed from the sprinklers hitting it for months or maybe years. The view through this window was reduced by 40 percent to 50 percent.

This was a very nice clubhouse and well-maintained. Obviously, they had tried to remove the alkaline film. I asked the bartender who was in charge of maintenance. He said it was the person's day off. I talked to him about the window problem and asked if I could do a test patch. He said that the window was a real problem and they were considering replacing it because nothing worked. Whatever I could do would be appreciated.

Alkalinity/calcium, a common problem with windows that are inundated with water, is neutralized and removed by acid. I suspected that they had tried acid and that it failed to work. First, I tried a phosphoric acid with no effect. Then I tried muriatic/hydrochloric acid and agitated it with a mild abrasive pad. No effect! In the back of my mind, I had one last chance product to try. However, I was very reluctant to use it.

This product was hydrofluoric acid (not hydrochloric acid), which is used to formulate a highly sophisticated painkiller. It is very dangerous. If you got any on your fingers, full strength, for instance, it could penetrate to the bone before you would feel it. We generally sold the product as an extreme toilet bowl cleaner. I was very cautious with this product because it was so hazardous. I put on rubber gloves and did the test patch. Wow! It worked fantastically! I created a clean area the size and shape of a ship's porthole. The bartender was duly impressed. I told him we would be back tomorrow.

The next day we saw the head of maintenance. He also was very impressed and wanted the product, now. I explained how hazardous the product was. He said he would store it in a safe place and handle it personally. He bought a few cases of it. Replacing that large glass window would certainly have cost hundreds, if not thousands, of dollars and the problem would have reoccurred. We came up with the perfect solution for them. In the end, it was not a huge sale, approximately $600, but very satisfying—plus the repeat business, of course.

Sales Call—Experience #4

"It always looked like that; it never looked good."

We continued to peruse the town, looking for potential qualified prospects. As we circled behind another major hotel, we noticed a terrazzo rear entryway. It was completely exposed to the weather with no overhead protection. First of all, terrazzo is great inside, but outside is a big mistake. Fortunately, it was in surprisingly good condition. I expected it to be corroded and badly worn. However, because of exposure to the weather, it was completely flat-looking and very dull, dirty, and unattractive.

The manager was in, and we were able to have a brief meeting with him. I told him that he had a first-class operation (which he did); however, the rear terrazzo entry was taking away from the good first impressions the hotel presented. His response was "It has always looked like that; it never looked good." Fortunately, I had a lot of experience with specialty floors like terrazzo. "Do you mind if we do a test patch to see if we can bring it back to life?" I asked. "Sure, go at it," he said.

That we did, first stripping a three-foot by three-foot test area with a solvent cleaner. It still looked dull, but it was now clean and stain-free. The next step was to coat it with a quick-drying solvent finish. The first coat looked good. After twenty minutes we applied a second coat. It now looked great. A third coat would have made it look fantastic, but we felt the additional time wasn't necessary, as it already looked really good!

We got the manager to come out and see it, and he could not believe it. He was blown away. "How did you do that?" he asked. It looked like we had cut out the three-foot-square test area and installed a brand-new section. "What do we have to do to get the rest of the floor looking like this?" he asked. I said that I could write an order for everything he would need. *(That statement was actually a subtle, low-pressure close.)* I said that if I could talk to his maintenance man now, I could go over the procedure with him and determine if he was capable or if he would need our help with the application. *(This was a second, reinforcing, low-pressure close. Any objections to the sale would come up now.)*

He called the maintenance man, and we had a meeting on how to do the floor. He actually was very knowledgeable. He knew exactly what to do. Problem: He was an unhappy employee and seemed to be bored to death and completely burned out! In sales, not only do you have to sell, but sometimes you also have to be a psychologist. This guy was a problem; if he did do the job, he would probably shortcut it, and we would have

an unhappy manager. I had an idea. I told the maintenance man how lucky he was!

"Wow," I said, "when you restore the floor and make it
look like this test patch, you will end up being the hero
that saved them the hundreds or thousands of dollars
it would have cost to replace it. They will probably
want to give you a medal or a raise or at least a bonus.
At any rate, you will be the man of the hour. What a
great opportunity for you. Afterward, depending on
what happens, that would be an excellent time to ask
for a raise." *That was the first time I saw him smile.*

I got ahold of the manager again, and in front of the
maintenance man, I told him how fortunate he was
to have someone with this man's knowledge and expertise, and I was confident that the floor would look
like new. We left with a $1,500 order. **Now we were
four for four.**

Sales Call—Experience #5

"You mean you are literally paying somebody to do this?"

We walked to the mall looking for a place to have lunch. We found a nice clean restaurant. Always being aware of any problems that we might encounter, I noticed that the floor was green-painted concrete. Most painted concrete floors don't look that good. This was the exception. They obviously maintained the floor by regularly applying a finish or a wax. However, indeed they did have a problem.

Six inches in from the wall, the floor was no longer green; it was black and very noticeable. This is not unusual because no one actually walks along the walls; therefore, the finish doesn't wear like the rest of the floor. After the initial two to three coats, you should never apply any additional wax or finish along the wall. Otherwise, you will soon have fifty to one hundred coats of buildup, such as what was staring us in the face!

I told the manager who we were and that we could sell him the product to strip the floor and give his maintenance man the necessary instructions to do the job. Or, if he liked, we also did maintenance and could strip the floor for him. His next statement caught me completely off guard. He said, "We have a cleaning company now." I blurted out, "You mean you are literally paying somebody to do this?" He folded his arms and looked into an empty space for approximately twenty seconds and then said to me, "How soon can you start?" **Five for five...**

Are you getting the picture?

Sales Call—Experience #6

A seriously risky demo paid off handsomely

The week of training ended, and the next day I was on my own again. (I've included this sale in my list of sales with my trainee because, even though he wasn't with me, it happened the very next day.) I called on a first-class health club in Encino, California. After a quick walk-through, I asked the manager about the white calcium buildup on his dark vinyl floor. He explained that the white residue buildup was caused by dripping water in the area that they called "the relaxing room," which was popular with members after using the showers and steam room. He said that they had tried a number of products and maintenance procedures, but nothing worked. So they decided to just live with it.

This was a unique problem. If we put a wax or water-based finish on the floor, the constant water problem would just dissolve it and compound the issue. What it needed was a solvent-based finish, impervious to water. The problem was, if the floor was vinyl asbestos or linoleum, solvent would certainly dissolve the floor.

This particular floor, however, appeared to have a quality vinyl tile structure. Even though I had never put a solvent finish on any resilient tile floor (it's dangerous to the floor), it seemed like a last-resort effort to solve the problem.

I explained the situation to the manager and asked him if I could do a small test on a couple of tiles. If the test looked good and there were no deleterious effects, I would wait a week to ensure that the test was secure. Then I would proceed with a larger test area. The manager was enthusiastic about my plan and gave the okay. The test tiles came out great! There was no noticeable damage, and they dried with a nice shine. The result was impressive.

A week later I did the second test, also successful. Then we applied what turned out to be a miracle finish for the club floor. Now they would be able to mop the water off the floor without leaving a white film. Needless to say, we secured the account for maintenance, as well as for all their supplies. They became one of my best maintenance accounts.

An interesting note: to restore the shine, we simple mopped the floor with a basic safety solvent. This re-emulsified the finish, and it looked as if we put down a fresh coat.

PMA

Remember, nothing can happen without it, especially for a salesperson. Without it, you might as well stay home! What is it? **Positive mental attitude!** It's critical that you are mentally prepared for the day. Make sure a PMA is with you when you leave the house!

The 80/20 Rule

The 80/20 rule dictates that 80 percent of the people just get by in life or simply fail. Also, 80 percent of start-up businesses fail in the first five years! What about the other 20 percent? These people take the initiative, think outside the box, and make things happen. They have lots of PMA.

What Is a Salesperson Anyway?

What usually comes to mind is the character in *Death of a Salesman*—the back-slapping, joke-telling, loud, laughing individual in a suit and tie. Those antics don't work in today's world. The true professional, successful salesperson is **simply being him- or herself, no façade,** and is always nicely dressed and well-groomed. He or she looks professional. The main difference between a salesperson and a wannabe salesperson is that he or she knows the product inside out and, more importantly, knows how to *close the sale!* **A salesperson who can't close is just a good conversationalist.**

Are You Just a Good Conversationalist?

It's simple: no close, no sale

Most salespeople can make a decent presentation and demonstration. Then, all of a sudden, they are dead in the water. It's psychological. They are waiting for the prospect to buy/order the product, and they just freeze. Salespeople like this are known as *order takers*.

"And the Blue Fairy Came Down…"

The average salesperson simply fails to close the sale. Therefore, the prospect now senses a way to put off the purchase/commitment. "Hey, I really like what you showed me. Leave me your card and brochure and I'll give you a call after I review everything." *(Sure, and then the blue fairy came down…)* The salesperson leaves with his tail between his legs. To that I say, "Hey, where are you going? You made it all the way to the two-yard line; at least make one more attempt to close. You have nothing to lose!"

For example: "Mr. Prospect, may I make a suggestion (soft close)? I know you were impressed with how well this product works, and I understand that you do not want to commit to a fifty-five-gallon drum, even though that's the most economical way to buy it. So, what if we start with just a couple five-gallon pails? That is just a small investment, and I'll throw in a couple of compression hand sprayers, which are usually only free with fifty-five-gallon drums. This will at least give you a chance to test the product under real circumstances.

"After you prove the product to yourself, you can order in larger quantities for the best discount. You know, we stand behind and guarantee our products. If you are not satisfied in any way, you can return them and pay nothing. So, with your okay, I'll send the two five-gallon pails, freight-free, and the two compression sprayers. Then I'll make it a point to stop by in a couple of weeks to make sure you are happy with the product. **What do you think? I really would like your business."**

If he still doesn't buy, try a similar close with just one five-gallon pail. Many times, by the time you get to this stage, the customer feels somewhat obligated to at least order the one five-gallon pail. You were ready to walk out without an order; you have now been given two additional chances to close and **move off the two-yard line for the touchdown.**

In that unbelievable week with my trainee, we really did not have to pressure any of our clients to close those sales (that's not my style). In almost every case, they more or less **asked us to sell them** whatever was necessary for the solution to their problem (a rarity). It's as if the excitement of seeing their problems eliminated, which they had been living with for who knows how long, easily created the momentum for them to take the next obvious step. These sales were solid, actually easy, once we solved their issue.

After rereading my earlier comments above, I recalled a sale that exemplifies exactly the situation as written above. I would like to interject that occurrence here.

This Salesman Was Dead in the Water

I received a lead for a commercial vacuum cleaner from one of the manufacturers we represented. It was for a small local airport. I did not have the vacuum in stock, so I asked the manufacturer to send out a representative to demo the vacuum that the prospect was interested in.

This representative made an impression on me. He was well-dressed in a suit and tie, well-groomed, and had a pleasant personality. He looked very professional. I expected to see a good demonstration. We called on the prospect, introduced ourselves, and the representative proceeded to demo the vacuum. As expected, the demo was smooth and professional, and the carpet looked great after the demo. At that stage, the customer was ready to buy. I expected the rep to close the sale.

Nay, nay, it never happened. Instead, they both sat down and started talking sports—football, baseball, and basketball. At first, I thought maybe he was just trying to warm up the prospect a bit before closing. That was not the case. *He was simply dead in the water.* I could not believe what was happening! I pictured the prospect soon saying, "Listen, I really have to get back to work. Why don't you leave me your card and brochure and I'll contact you." *(Blue fairy?)*

They sat talking for fifteen minutes. I became increasingly frustrated. I have seen this exact situation many times with my trainees and the competition, too. Metaphorically, I saw the sale headed for the cliff, soon to drop over, crash, and burn. I jumped in for the rescue to save the sale.

"So, Mr. Prospect, I'm over here looking at the carpet we just vacuumed. Is this the result you were after?"

"Yes. It really looks good!"

"We won't be able to leave this vacuum with you, but we will be happy to send you a new one in approximately one week" (first soft close).

"I really could use that vacuum; it's just what we need. However, my wife handles all the financing, and she would have to approve it."

"I understand. Is your wife on the premises now?"

"Yes, she is in the back office."

"May I go back to her office for her approval?" (second close). The assumption in that statement was that he was going to buy it. I didn't ask him if he wanted to buy it. He would have assumed that I thought he wanted to buy it. (Any objections would come up at this point.)

In her office, I said, "Your husband says that this is exactly what he needs and would like to purchase it, but he says that is your department."

"I know he has talked about the need for a new vacuum, but our finances are a little tight now."

"May I make a suggestion? Our billing is thirty days. If that puts a strain on your finances, we can spread it out over ninety days, in this case. This commercial vacuum sells for a thousand dollars. If you can write me a check for a third today, I can get the order processed. Then you can follow up with a check for another third each of the next two months." (If there was any objection from the wife, it would have come up now.)

"Yes, I know that would make him happy. Let me write you a check."

That is just how it happened. Sale saved—the end. (No blue fairy here.)

Yes, that may have been a little strong, but at that stage, an order was questionable, and once you leave without the order, chances for writing that order in the future are slim. Taking a strong initiative at that time was absolutely the right action, and for that reason, we did end up with the order after all. (Case closed!)

What this salesman experienced is not unusual as discussed previously. It takes perseverance and practice to move out of the "fear of closing" mentality.

Here is a simple close, which I have used a few times: "Mr. Prospect, if you can give me an okay, I'll go ahead and ship the order." Continuing without hesitation (you don't want any negatives at this stage), "Then I'll stop back to show your man, Joe, the proper cleaning technique." A little humor may also help: "I know you like the vacuum for your operation; should I send in one for you and maybe another three or four for your friends and relatives?" Probable answer: "No thanks, one will be plenty/enough."

If you feel the sale is lost, think outside the box. What do you have to lose at this stage? Be creative and offer or say something, even if you think it's risky. Again, you have nothing to lose. Further on in this book, I tell of a time when I was sure the sale was lost, so I said to the buyer, "You are the toughest lady executive housekeeper I have ever called on." I thought she might be insulted by this statement, but instead, she unexpectedly took that as a compliment. Then she opened up and I ended up writing an order.

Again, It's Simple:
No Close, No Sale!

Now follow me here: The ordinary salesperson has to make an extraordinary amount of calls in order to make the same amount of money that the extraordinary salesperson makes with an ordinary amount of calls. *However, using our method, the ordinary salesperson automatically becomes the extraordinary salesperson by making only qualified (fewer) calls.*

Six Out of Six Calls

Okay, time to fess up. I was not completely truthful when I said we sold six out of seven calls, and I am having a difficult time writing the following: *we sold six out of six calls!* The above statement was the result of a heated discussion with my very wise daughter.

She said, "Dad, why don't you just state what really happened? You did sell six out of six, not six out of seven."

My answer: "Honey, it just isn't credible. That doesn't happen in the real world; nobody will believe it."

"It is the truth, though. If they don't want to believe it, so be it!"

She won the debate, hence the above correction.

Actually, you can simply prove everything I wrote in this book for yourself. Go out and look for the problems (no more unqualified calls). If you wish to cover an area with cold calls, be alert for problems within each call and proceed with a demonstration, when possible. You will most likely end up with a sale. Think outside the box when necessary and *always close.* (Or you risk the blue fairy coming down.)

As I mentioned earlier, when I thought back over my years of sales, I realized that I was always more successful when I solved a problem. When I started out, I made call after call like any other cold call salesman, and I sold an average of one out of three qualified customers. Sometimes, however, you have to make as many as five to ten calls just to see enough prospects to sell one out of three. The prospect may be out or just too busy to see you, etc. But after a week in the field, we confirmed that the key to qualifying the sale was finding the prospect's problem. **All those wasted calls are eliminated! (We proved it!)**

At the end of this book, I will include an in-depth explanation of the pluses that aided us during our incredible week of sales calls and help you to implement your own successful sales plan, as well. I will also cover any negatives that can hinder you. I have included my contact information at the end of the book for questions or answers to sales challenges or just additional information.

Making the Close — Hard or Soft

As I think back over my years in sales, I have noted some of my more interesting and sometimes humorous sales. All of my sales exemplify the sales close. The sales close can be soft; it does not have to be hard or high pressure. You don't have to feel that you have to be strong and get that sale at all costs. *(That scares a lot of salespeople from even attempting the close.)*

You can still take the initiative and make a soft close. This can be an alternative close, such as "Do you see a particular color that you like?" This is often used as an example by sales trainers. Not a black and white close, but in the right direction.

Here is a better one, a bit more aggressive but still somewhat soft. "Now that you can see how nice the test patch looks, I would be happy to write an order for covering the entire floor. Then I'll come back and help your man apply it correctly and the floor should turn out beautiful. If you like the idea, is there a good day to meet with your maintenance man? I'm free either Monday or Tuesday. Would either of those days be good?" His answer of either Monday or Tuesday means he is sold, so write up the order.

If you noticed in my sales calls, I was always willing to work with the customer's maintenance man, whether it was at night, on Sunday, during a holiday, or at 3:00 a.m. Whatever it takes to make the sale—or not. Your choice. **The customer is also impressed with this "outside the box" type of commitment.** Later in the book, I talk about my 3:00 a.m. sales call.

My Ten-Word Close Resulted in a $2,000 Sale

We had our first trade show in Canada, in Montreal, Quebec. It was actually in the underground part of the convention hall. It was a huge, very impressive show, with hundreds of booths and thousands of people. Our company, U.S. Products, was displaying its line of colored shampoo tanks and heated carpet cleaners, as well as upholstery/drapery cleaning equipment.

One attendee had placed an order for shampoo tanks, and before he left, he spotted our heated wet- and dry-cleaning upholstery equipment. He was somewhat intrigued with what he saw, so I walked him through the features. Now he was even more intrigued and crouched down to get a better view. I crouched down with him. We stayed in that position for a few minutes. At this stage, he seemed very impressed with the equipment. I was sensing his extreme interest and the timing seemed right for my next statement (*ten-word close*), **"Do you want me to add one to your order?"** He said, "Yes, why don't you?" Timing and sales instincts played a big part in this sale. Some salespeople have it naturally; some develop it over time.

The Ultimate Model PBIII, our unique upholstery/drapery cleaning machine

Show Note: My Wife's Suggestion Turned into a Major Source of Business

Before the show started, my wife said to me, "Why don't we give away candy at the booth?" I really was not that impressed with the idea. I said, "A lot of exhibitors give away candy, but if you want to, fine." *It was quite a bit better than just fine, as I would discover.*

Most exhibitors would just set a candy dish close to the aisle and attendees were free to pick up whatever they wanted. Be aware, the show was big, and most attendees would just walk right by your booth, unless they came specifically to see your line or were existing customers who wanted to find out about your show specials.

My wife was a nice-looking lady, and the candy that she was giving out was very desirable: chocolates, mini candy bars, etc. Now, picture this: my wife would stand in the middle of the aisle and as an attendee walked by, she would place the candy dish in front of him or her and ask if he or she wanted some goodies for the trip back home. At least 90 percent of the time, they stopped for the candy and a pleasant conversation with this attractive lady.

I would then walk up during their conversation and say, "Are you familiar with our line? We have some unique products. Let me show you a couple of our popular items."

With this routine, my wife stopped almost everyone she approached, and we had dozens of people who were just passing by stop and come into our booth. The result was a lot of extra business. ***The prospect who purchased the $2,000 upholstery machine was someone who was just walking by.*** After that, we employed this procedure at all of our trade shows.

Time for a little sales humor: The new salesman was bragging that he got three orders the very first day: **Get out, stay out, and never come back.**

This salesperson says to his prospect: **Close your eyes and sign this order and I will send you more merchandise than you have ever seen in your life.**

Okay, that's it, back to work.

As Elmer Wheeler, Noted Author, Says,

"Sell the sizzle, not the steak."

During my early sales career, before I opened my first business, I worked for Whitehall Laboratories, an international pharmaceutical company that also manufactured a line of proprietary products. I called on drugstores and supermarkets. This reputable company spent millions in advertising, and many of their products were well-known.

One of my accounts was a major chain drugstore. I wanted to sell the manager on the idea of putting up an end display of our Kolynos toothpaste. An end display in a supermarket or super drugstore usually increased sales by 300 percent to 500 percent as long as the display was up. I came up with a unique creation to help sell the idea.

My wife helped me build a six-foot offset tower from two hundred empty toothpaste cartons. Then I built a box with a three-RPM motor inside to make the tower turn slowly. Revolving the tower of toothpaste made it look like something that Disney would come up with. It was very impressive. Then we put flashing lights in red and blue on both sides of the display and topped it off with a crown advertising the toothpaste at the top of the tower. We then built an imitation end display and filled it with more empty toothpaste cartons. It looked just like the real thing. We took pictures, and I was now ready to make my presentation.

Here was my dilemma: this toothpaste was not as heavily advertised as the rest of the line. If I was selling a major brand like Colgate, that product was heavily advertised and deserved the space necessary for an end display. How was I going to justify putting up an end display of my toothpaste?

I made an appointment with the manager. *(Here comes the sizzle.)* I showed him the photo and explained that this was a new original display. I told him that these displays were going to be in demand, and I was fortunate enough to have one in my inventory. (The amount of demand was speculation on my part but came to pass as I predicted.) I added that I knew that the supply of these displays was going to be very limited and they would be put up on a first come, first served basis. This was true since I was the one in control.

I then explained the uniqueness of this display. I said to him, "It's a six-foot revolving tower that would be spotted immediately by everyone entering the store. This looks like a Disney creation, and the kids will be dragging their parents over to see the display." The Kolynos 2/69 toothpaste pack was very well designed and looked like it was created just for this promotional end display, which further enhanced the effect.

"Mr. Manager (beginning of soft close), to be truthful, I have been pondering which one of my customers would benefit the most from this display and could move the most merchandise. (Close continued) I have six hundred accounts in my territory and have come up with just a handful of prospects, and that's why I am here. You are at the top of my list! (True, they were my largest account, a Sav-On drugstore.) This is a unique, one-of-a-kind display, and you will have the first and only one in the L.A. metropolitan area. (Simple, low pressure close) If you like what you see and can give me an order now <u>to guarantee the display's availability</u>, I'll make arrangements to install it."

"How much do I have to order?"

Now, I was under a little pressure. We offered the Kolynos toothpaste in chlorophyll and white. They only moved a couple dozen of the chlorophyll and three dozen of the white per month. I needed a quantity order for this to be successful. Trying to be matter-of-fact, I said, "Oh, a gross (144) of the chlorophyll and a couple gross (288) of the white."

With very little hesitation he said, "Okay, send it in."

Kolynos toothpaste display

Phenomenal success! The outcome was all that I had hoped for. The customers swarmed around the revolving tower display. The kids loved it. The manager was thrilled. As rewarding as this was, the "proof in the pudding" was how much merchandise we sold. The average good display can have an increase in sales of 300 percent to 500 percent. We had an amazing 800 percent to 1,000 percent increase in sales! I reported the results to headquarters.

In the next company letter, they gave me credit. Bernie Gurstein has a 600 percent increase in Kolynos toothpaste sales. I guess a 600 percent increase was more credible. This relates to my earlier statement of six out of seven, instead of six out of six sales.

This is not a fact, but I assume that our display sold more toothpaste than anyone in the history of the company. All it takes is thinking out of the box, being creative, and doing some hard work—or not. (And, of course, my wife's help.)

An interesting after-the-sale experience: I was observing/analyzing our display when a representative from another major toothpaste company approached me with a look of consternation on his face. He blurted out, "How the hell did you get that display up? You don't deserve that kind of space!"

I was really taken aback. If the situation were re-versed, I would have said, "Hey, nice job, good sale." I think that most professional salespeople would have responded likewise. I guess he was just upset that I up-ended him and took the display space that he thought should have been his.

My answer was short. "You are right. I didn't deserve the space, so it must have been my superior salesman-ship." And I walked away.

There's the Logical Reason for Not Buying

and then there is the real reason

Just like a typical politician, the potential customer will give you a logical reason why he or she can't buy: "We need to take a thorough inventory at this time to evaluate our financial situation," or "Taxes are coming up soon and we are reducing our purchases until it's over," or "We are remodeling and holding off until we know the cost," etc.

Then there is the real reason: he wants to buy a super expensive sports car, or he has a mistress he is supporting on the side, or he simply does not like you. Whatever the excuse, the point is that the prospect will present a logical reason for not buying, and then there is the *real* reason.

This is really a tough one and I don't have the perfect salesperson's comeback. This calls for on-the-spot creativity—possibly an extra 20 percent off "today only," or free goods "today only." You simply have to play this type of situation by ear. If you have a good demonstrable product, that could make the difference.

How Your Company Name
Can Greatly Enhance
Your Profit Margin

So, exactly what can a name do for your company? *Plenty!* Depending what the name is, of course.

My first experience with the benefit of our company's name was when our operation was brand new and I called the first supplier with whom I wanted to establish an account. After a short introduction, I said that I was interested in an open account with his company and asked what kind of dating was available. He said, "What is the name of your company?" I replied, "U.S. Research & Chemical." He said, "Oh, thirty days." So, just on the strength of our name, we opened an account with thirty-day billing and no credit reports or verification of any kind.

In sales, if you cannot get in to see the prospect in the first place, then of course, there is no presentation and no opportunity to make a sale. This is where our company name was so valuable. My business card only had our name on it running through an outline of the United States. Under the company name was my name with "representative." No description or hint of what U.S. Research & Chemical was or did. Why? Read on.

When calling on a major company, you try to get an appointment. Many times, they screen you on the phone and you can't get an appointment. My technique was to make a cold call on the account, and when the secretary asked what my business was, I would say, "I am here to see 'Mr. Prospect.' Would you give him my card please?"

If I got this far, and she actually took my card to show the man, the chances were he would come out to meet me. Why? Because the card didn't give him any information about what the company was or who I was or why I was calling on him. However, the name "U.S. Research & Chemical" is impressive and he'd be curious. What is this company and why are they calling on me? I have found in most cases he would come out to meet me.

Again, the credibility of our name alone often got us into the presentation and/or demonstration.

This is where you follow the procedure outlined further on in the book for **"how to get into nine out of ten doors!"** At the end of your introductory presentation, believe me, the prospect will be very curious and will want to know more about the product or service you are talking about. **The whole idea of this section was to get you to this stage!** Now it's all up to you. Hopefully, you are well prepared to make a dramatic presentation on why your product is going to save him time and money or some other major benefit. Do you have documentation, testimonies, or the actual product, if it can be demonstrated?

What Is a Unit? Whatever You Want It to Be!

How it made this close more effective

I remember one account that I called on. The only name I had was the president's. I gave my card to the secretary, and she gave it to the president. Just like it was supposed to, the card piqued his curiosity and he came out to see who U.S. Research & Chemical was.

Before this point, when I was driving up to the account, I had noticed fifty-five-gallon drums all over the premises. This was a concrete company, and I was presenting a product that prevented the concrete from sticking to the trucks, making it faster and more efficient to clean and restore them to like-new, professional-looking trucks.

This was an expensive product, and if I was talking to a smaller company, I might be suggesting five-gallon pails. In this case, however, I knew they purchased mainly in fifty-five-gallon drums. So, when it came to the close, I referred to our product as **units of 55-gallon drums.** I suggested he start with three units (not 165 gallons) for the very best price. He ended up buying just one unit (a fifty-five-gallon drum). It was easier to say yes to only one unit, and I was very happy with this multi-hundred-dollar sale.

Usually, most of these types of companies buy in quantity, and the sales that I did make were very profitable.

The Only Caveat Is
It's a 3 a.m. Sales Call...

Whatever it takes to make the sale!

I had a good distributor in Las Vegas, and he sold a lot of our equipment to the hotels. On one call to his operation, he asked me if I would make a presentation of our high-pressure carpet steam cleaner to one of the hotels. I said, "Sure, be happy to." The only caveat was that it was for the night shift and we would have to make the call at three in the morning.

I was sure he was kidding. "No," he said, "I'm not kidding. It's for the night crew, and that's the only time they can schedule us in." I said, "That would be a first for me, but so be it."

He said, "Bernie, I'm impressed. Over the years when I have asked other manufacturers to make a middle-of-the-night call, I would usually get turned down." I answered, "Well, if we make a sale, we both benefit. So tell me when and where and I'll be there."

I don't remember exactly which hotel it was, but it was one of the major ones on the strip. There was nothing unique or outstanding about this call, other than it was at three in the morning. The point being, if you want to stand out and be successful, these are some of the things you have to do. I certainly stood out in my distributor's eyes. Our relationship was much improved after that call, and by the way, yes, we had a good demonstration and we did make the sale.

"Bob, You Just Can't Keep Coming in Every Weekend— Make a Decision!"

I said earlier in the book that high pressure isn't my style and I prefer low pressure. I was exasperated with this prospect, however, so this was the exception. Even though I was strong with this prospect, it was still done in a lighthearted manner and was successful. Here is how it went down…

"Bob" came into our store/shop one weekend to look at the window cleaning equipment. He was considering going into the window cleaning business. I walked him through the equipment and said that I would help him get started and to think of me as his coach. I spent thirty to forty-five minutes with him. He thanked me and said he would think about it.

The next weekend he came into the store again. We basically repeated the same scenario as the previous week. Again, he said he would think about it and left. Yes, you may have guessed it—the next weekend he came in again for a repeat of the last two weekends.

When he came in on the fourth weekend, I started

trying to analyze what was with this guy. Obviously, he was very interested in going into the window cleaning business. He just was having a very hard time making a decision.

He was standing in front of the window cleaning display. I walked up to him and said, "Bob, I know you want to go into the window cleaning business, and yes, it's a tough decision and does involve some risk, but you simply have to make a commitment, either yes or no. I'm going to help you with that decision."

I gently grabbed him by the collar, looked him in the eye, and said, "Bob, buy the equipment to get into the window cleaning business. Now. Today! It will come to approximately two hundred dollars. There will be zero risk on your part. If it doesn't work out, just return the equipment and I will happily give you a one-hundred percent refund. We will still be friends. You will go your way and I, my way.

"I have never, ever, offered anyone what I'm offering you today. Just give me a yes and I'll write up the order and you will finally be in the window cleaning business!" He gave me a yes, with a big smile on his face.

In the final analysis, he simply needed someone like me to push him in the right direction. By the way, his business did become successful. He even added carpet cleaning to his business, and he purchased the carpet cleaning equipment from us. Over the years of doing business, we became good friends.

"Why Did You Hurt That Nice Young Man?"

"Honey, I didn't hurt him; I actually helped him."

One day a manufacturer's sales representative called on me at my store to present his line of aerosol products. He was a young man, well-groomed and professional. However, this turned out to be a very short sales call, and the rep left without an order.

Here is what transpired: After the presentation of his products, which was somewhat lacking but adequate, I intended to draw him out a little and see how he reacted. So, I said, *"Tell me why I should buy from you."* Unfortunately, he became flustered and left without an order.

In answer to my wife's question, I told her the reason I didn't hurt him but actually helped him was that any decent salesperson would have easily answered me with at least three or more good reasons to buy from him. When this salesman got back to his car, I'm sure that he started thinking about the many reasons why future prospects should buy from him. Again, this either helped him become a better-prepared salesman or made him realize that he wasn't cut out for sales.

How NOT to Get In to Nine Out of Ten Calls

Actually, this is not a bad presentation, but if you do not get the intended results, it still makes no difference. "Good morning, Mr. Prospect, I'm Bernie Gurstein with U.S. Research & Chemical. We are a complete janitorial/sanitary supply house. I realize that you probably already have a source of supply and that you are probably happy with your source.

"Since your business is relatively close to our operation, we are in a unique position to offer you same-day delivery, or when necessary, we are only fifteen minutes away, making it easy for one of your people to make a quick pickup. We have a complete line of vacuum and floor equipment. We also carry a line of cleaning chemicals and floor finishes.

"We can also handle any repairs of your equipment. (Soft close) If you happen to be in need of any supplies today, I would be happy to take your order, and that would give you a chance to test our service."

Not a bad presentation, really, and on occasion you probably would write some business. However, this would be the typical response: "Hey, Bernie, sounds like you have a nice operation. Why don't you leave your card and brochure? I'll look it over and possibly give you a call." (Blue fairy time)

Now, How to GET IN to Nine Out of Ten Calls

You will be impressed at how effective this is!

"Good morning, Mr. Prospect, I'm Bernie Gurstein with U.S. Research & Chemical. We are a complete janitorial/sanitary supply house. I realize that you probably already have a source of supply and that you are probably happy with your source. However, most supply houses generally are competitive and carry similar lines.

"We are different in that we look for and offer specialty products that are not available from our competition. I'm calling on you today to present such a product. If you have five minutes for my presentation, I'll show you what I have."

At this stage, they are not going to say, "I'm sorry, I'm too busy right now." No, definitely not, you have aroused their curiosity. "Okay, let's see what you have" is the most common answer. Now that you have their attention, you want to present your most unique product.

In one instance, though, the prospect came out to the lobby to see me and seemed rushed. After my standard introductory presentation, he was curious to know what I had, but he just stood there, wanting to see it right then and there in the lobby. If you encounter a similar situation, you can do what I did. "Mr. Prospect, thank you for coming out to see me, but this is too important to just make a rushed presentation in the lobby. Can we go back to your office? If you don't have time for that now, maybe I'll just come back another day." He actually apologized and said, "Can you come back about two o'clock today? Then you can have as much time as you need."

Impressive Demo Products

One of my favorite products that helped me get in the door when calling on any company that depends on vehicles, such as taxicabs, ambulances, police cars, etc. was a product that displaced moisture. It worked by its molecular tension. I would have a small electric motor with me. I would spray the motor with this product and its molecular tension would cause the product to defy gravity and move up and down, penetrating and enveloping all surfaces. The motor was now waterproof! I would have a small pail with me that I would fill with water and submerge the motor. The next move is hard to believe, but I would plug the motor into a 110-volt electrical outlet. It would run smoothly, churning up the water without shorting out. Sometimes I would end up with five to ten employees watching the demonstration.

Next, we would go out to one of their vehicles. When I called on the Los Angeles police department, I did this exact demonstration described above. When we went out to one of their police vehicles, with their permission, I lifted the hood, took off the distributor cap (before digital ignitions), and sprayed water into the distributor. We then attempted to start it. Of course, it would not start. I took off the distributor cap again and sprayed the moisture displacement product into the distributor, closed the hood, and said, "Okay, start it up." I was sweating a little bit at that stage, but sure enough, it started up. They bought several cases to outfit all of their vehicles. If you are interested in this product, I assume you can locate one on the internet under "moisture displacement products." The Thomas Register is also a good source for products and suppliers.

I had another favorite, which was a safety solvent that would not conduct electricity. It was very useful in machine shops, repair shops, or wherever a lot of electrical equipment was in operation. I would take a small plastic pail, fill it with safety solvent, and submerge my small electric motor into the solvent and plug it into a 110-volt circuit. While it was running submerged, *I would put my hand inside the solvent to show that it was safe and would not electrocute me.* Very, very impressive but scary demonstration.

It was used for spraying into electric motors, switches, etc. Some janitorial supply houses carry a product like this now. Since it is a solvent, it can also be sold as a dry-cleaning product or spotter. We sold it with our dry-cleaning drapery/upholstery machine. These products usually have a high flash point and that's why it's referred to as a safety solvent.

Although these products are unique and impressive, you can take any product in your line and look for the advantages that the competition does not have. Another example follows.

Selling Quality Over Price

A contract cleaner came into our store looking for a good floor finish. I presented our best floor finish, Thermoshield. As I mentioned before, product names and descriptions are very important. We sold a lot of this finish because, with a name like that, it sounded high-tech and, therefore, it just had to be good.

Our high-quality floor finish "Thermoshield"

This prospect had a nice-sized company but was cost-conscious and thought that my product was a bit pricey. He thought he could probably save a couple dollars a gallon from my competition.

I said, "Really? Let me ask you some questions about my competitor's product. Is the color amber to brown?" He answered yes. "If you look at our product, you will notice that it is white, which means that it's highly refined and pure. The darker the color, the less refined it is and the risks of imperfections and problems increase. Also, Thermoshield was designed to break down when stripped with an ammoniated stripper. Ammonia helps break down most finishes; however, our finish is formulated to react faster and more efficiently, which saves labor and therefore money.

"Do you know what the solids for that finish are? Ours are twenty percent, which is as concentrated as you want in a floor finish, and that determines the base cost of the finish. We can add as much water as you want to make the product as cheap as you want. *How cheap do you want it?* With all the advantages of Thermoshield, which also includes longer durability, high gloss, and a high anti-slip factor, just two dollars a gallon more is a fair and real value."

He purchased a five-gallon pail to test and became a good customer of Thermoshield for many years!

Another good example was at our trade shows. Many times contract cleaners would come into our booth to see our heavily advertised carpet steam cleaners. One popular model was our Cobra. Sometimes we got the comment, "It's a bit pricey, isn't it?"

My answer, and this should be your answer too if your product is a quality one and the value is there: "What do you mean pricey? This is the least

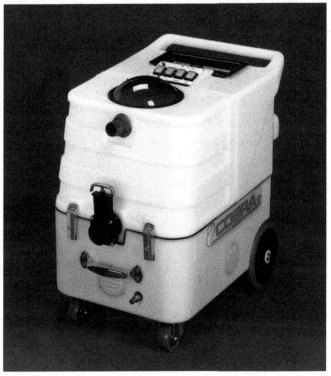

High-heat/high PSI carpet cleaning "Cobra"

expensive machine that you can buy on the market today! We didn't invent the 'heat exchanger,' but we were the first manufacturer to put one inside a carpet steam cleaner, giving us the capability of cleaning at two hundred degrees at the spray tip. In addition, our 300-PSI pump is a huge plus. It's like having a truck mount in a portable.

"Some interesting things happen at two hundred degrees. For instance, your cleaning efficiency goes up two hundred percent, and many spots and stains come out with hot water that would not normally come out. However, the real value is evident when you start cleaning. If you are cleaning at the rate of one thousand square feet per hour now, with the increased cleaning efficiency and high heat, your cleaning speed will increase to between fifteen hundred and two thousand square feet per hour, depending on the type of carpet and its age and condition. Besides our normal one-year warranty, we also have a lifetime warranty on the body.

"So, now, cleaning at up to double the carpet that you are currently, **you can see where the increase in efficiency makes this the least expensive machine you can buy!"**

This presentation sells a lot of machines at these trade shows.

Hopefully, these examples will help in choosing a product to present and demonstrate. You can see that by picking a product from your line that stands out and highlighting all the advantages—anticipating all the objections and making a professional demonstration, if called for—your sales and business will grow accordingly.

The Most Unforgettable, Exasperating, Frustrating,

humiliating, emotional sales call in my entire sales career!

I made this call while I was still employed by Whitehall Laboratories, before I started my own business. Whitehall was well-known and manufactured popular products like Anacin, Dristan, Preparation H, etc.

It all started with a call on a large independent drug-store customer. I was in a good mood as I walked into the store, but that was short-lived. As I entered the store, I sensed something foreboding and I became apprehensive. It was like ESP. I had never experienced anything like this before. This was a huge drugstore, and as I looked around, I saw that there was not one customer in the entire store. I realized that wherever the bad feeling was coming from, it was driving all the customers out of the store.

I was now alert and on guard for whatever might come up. I proceeded as I normally would. "Good morning, Mr. Jones, Whitehall Laboratories. Is it okay to take an inventory?"

Acknowledging that he said okay, I proceeded to take an inventory of our products. Next, I showed him the suggested order for stock, then the specials and "deals" for his approval. So far, so good, I thought, although I was still apprehensive and cautious.

In presenting the inventory and specials/deals, I sensed that I needed to be as professional as possible and straightforward, and then just get out of there. Nay, nay, here's what happened...

We had a special on Preparation H. We were introducing Preparation H suppositories, and when the customer ordered two dozen of the ointment, he was entitled to an extra 10 percent off on the suppositories.

"Mr. Jones," I said, "we have a special on our new Preparation H suppositories. You have to order two dozen ointment..." I was going to continue, "in order to get the extra ten percent on the suppositories." But he never let me get that far. I got as far as "You have to order two dozen ointment..." **That's when the world came to an end.**

He was a big man, and with all his power, he slammed his palm down on the counter, yelling and screaming at me *in my face:* **"What do you mean I have to order two dozen ointment? I don't have to order anything!"**

I was really shocked and taken aback. He grabbed my

pencil in his hand like you would hold a knife. Then, with very heavy strokes, he crossed out my suggested order.

He was out of control at that point. I was fearful that he might stab me with the pencil. I immediately walked out from behind the counter, backed off about twenty paces, and turned to face him.

He continued his tirade yelling, ***"Who do you think you are? Just because you work for a large company you think you can come in here and tell me what to do?"***

As I mentioned earlier in the book, part of sales, sometimes, is being a psychologist. So I just stood there for two or three minutes letting him vent. I didn't take it personally. I thought maybe his wife had cheated on him or wanted a divorce, or maybe he'd lost a lot of money. It could have been anything.

After a while, he started calming down a bit. At that point, something humorous popped into my mind. Recently I had seen a movie where the wife was trying to convince her husband to tell her what was bothering him. "Honey," she said, "I promise, I won't be upset with you. I'll be calm; just get it off your chest." He replied, "Okay, I'll tell you. I had an affair with my secretary." The very next scene was a Japanese zero warplane making a suicidal crash dive.

Meanwhile, Mr. Jones was through venting and I saw an opening. "Listen, Mr. Jones, I really would like to apologize; you are absolutely right. Of course, you do not have to order anything that you don't want. That was a little insensitive of me. What I meant to say is if you ordered two dozen ointment, you would be qualified for the extra ten percent off. I have been calling on you for a couple years now, Mr. Jones, and we have always had a good relationship, so again, I'm really sorry for this misunderstanding."

He was quiet for a second and then responded gruffly, "Send it in."

"Thanks so much, Mr. Jones. See you next trip."

Afterward I treated myself to some coffee and a goodie, and then I took the rest of the day off.

In the final analysis of that call, if I hadn't kept my cool and had tried to defend myself by yelling back at him, I probably would have lost a good account along with the order and my commission, as well.

The Salesman Grabbed
Him and Threatened Him

I thought, "What an idiot, he just cut his own throat."

This was a cold call on a convalescent hospital in Van Nuys, California. The administrator was on the phone, so I took a seat and waited for him to finish. His call dragged on and on. While waiting, I noticed his maintenance man was cleaning the windows in the lobby where I was seated. I was bored waiting, so I started to pay more attention to the maintenance man's cleaning technique.

What I soon realized was that he had no technique, was cleaning with a "Mickey Mouse" twelve-inch cheapie squeegee, and really had no clue how to clean windows. I knew the administrator could see me as I walked over to offer some tips on window cleaning, and that could be a plus for me. However, even if the administrator had not seen what I was doing, I still would have offered my help.

The maintenance man seemed to appreciate my assistance. I showed him basic window cleaning strokes to eliminate streaking and how to be more efficient. I explained that most of the problem was his poor equipment and that I would speak to Mr. Herman, the administrator, about it. He thanked me and I went back to waiting.

Finally, Mr. Herman finished his call and I was able to introduce myself. After my introduction, I got into the problems that the maintenance man was having with the windows. He said, "I noticed you helping him, thanks."

"Not a problem," I said, "but he is working with inferior equipment, and that is a major handicap. That twelve-inch squeegee is highly inefficient and is taking considerably longer than need be, besides causing poor results. What you need is a professional twenty-inch brass window squeegee, a professional window brush, and a good concentrated window cleaner. (Now, the well-timed, simple close.) If you give me the okay, I'll send in the order, then come back and teach your man how to clean windows like a professional. With the right equipment and instructions, your man will clean twice the windows he is doing now, with fewer streaks and superior results." He saw the logic and agreed. "Send it in."

I now had a reason to come back. After I returned and showed his maintenance man how to do windows professionally, I was able to present another product, our Thermoshield floor finish to Mr. Herman, and he ended up purchasing a five-gallon pail to test. After they tested the five-gallon pail, they were impressed enough to order a thirty-gallon drum.

At this stage, however, a problem with a competitive salesman developed. I don't want to mention any names here, but he was not professional. In fact, I would call him underhanded. This salesman called our company, passing himself off as a representative of the convalescent hospital, and canceled the thirty-gallon order. Not only was he underhanded, but obviously, by his actions, he also was panicky and in fear of losing the account, which he had reason to be.

I stopped by the hospital to see why the order was canceled and uncovered the truth. Then I stopped in to see Jose, the maintenance man. He appeared upset, and I asked him what the problem was. It seems that my competitor stopped by to see him and demanded that Jose only order from him and nobody else. He drove home the message by grabbing Jose by the collar. I thought, "What an idiot, he just cut his own throat."

I asked Jose if he had told Mr. Herman, the administrator. In broken English, he said, "No, I no want to cause trouble." I told Jose, "That's okay; don't worry about it. I'll tell Mr. Herman what happened."

I stopped by Mr. Herman's office to inform him of

what had transpired. He was also taken aback by this representative's actions. Needless to say, that was the end of my competition.

Mr. Herman then surprised me with a question out of the blue: "Bernie, do you know why I started to do business with you?" I quipped, *"It was probably my good looks and charming personality."* We both chuckled. "Of course," I thought to myself, "I know exactly why." I didn't tell him though.

He answered, "I was impressed that you wanted to help Jose with the window cleaning." I said, "I'm glad that it worked out for the both of us, and Jose, too!"

The moral of this sale is don't do what my competitor did, running scared and using underhanded methods (which never work). He should have been more professional. Here is what I (or any good salesperson, for that matter) would have done if the situation were reversed:

Have a meeting with the administrator and, being very direct, say, "Mr. Herman, I have been doing business with you for a little while now, and I thought that my products were working well for you and that our prices were competitive. Jose seemed happy too, but now I see products from my competition. Are you unhappy with me, or my products, or the pricing? I have worked hard to make sure you are satisfied, and I value your business, as well as our relationship. So, Mr. Herman, is there anything that I can do or correct at this stage to at least keep some of your business, if not all of it?"

There is a good chance that he would feel somewhat guilty about cutting me off completely. The possibility of still doing some business is good after a presentation like that.

My Magic "Abracadabra" Sale

The problem was eliminated
as fast as you can say ...

One afternoon, a lady walked into my store with a
small rug. The rug was tan in color, but in the center
was a six- to eight-inch round, super bright orange
stain. I said, "It looks like you spilled some bowl cleaner on your rug."

She responded, "That's exactly what happened. How
did you know?"

I answered, "Well, that small oval-shaped rug looks
like it came out of a bathroom, and the stain looks like
a chemical change type of stain, which is how an acid
bowl-cleaner spill could react."

To neutralize an acid stain, which has a pH as low as
one to three, you would use a product with a pH of
approximately ten to twelve. At this stage, I was just
making an educated guess. Yes, I could have taken
an actual pH test and been more precise; however, I
did not have that capability at the time. Remarkably,
my guess was right on. I used one of my cleaning products that had a higher pH of ten to eleven,
called Blazethru. I sprayed Blazethru fully onto the
stain and the reaction was textbook. Literally, within

one to two seconds, the orange stain completely disappeared—*abracadabra.*

The lady reacted with "Wow! That's the most fantastic cleaner I have ever seen!" As a professional, I could not let her think that my cleaner deserved all the credit. So I explained to her about the pH reaction and said, "As good a cleaner as Blazethru is, I probably would have gotten the same reaction with just ammonia, which also has a high pH."

Her reaction was "I don't care. I want two gallons of that Blazethru." After my explanation, I thought that I might lose the sale, but see, it pays to be honest.

After that episode, I was really taken aback and impressed. You might say, "Why? That's your business; you are used to those experiences." Yes, I have neutralized acid spills on floors and alkaline spills, too. I have also taken stains out of upholstery by using either acid- or alkaline-based stain removers. But the results are never quite that dramatic. The stains don't change color like the bathroom rug; they just disappear. The floors don't change color either; they just become neutralized. This was the first time in my sales career that I experienced such a dramatic reaction. As they say, "You learn something new every day."

The "Shit and Piss" Sale

Sounds crass, I know, but it was what it was—funny

This very beautiful lady walked into our store one day and caught everyone off guard. She looked like a movie star—statuesque, well-dressed, long blond hair, and very high heels —the complete package. Both my employees and the customers turned to stare.

I greeted her, "Good morning, may I help you?" (Everybody was following her every move.) She was a foreigner, and with broken English she said, "I want something to take the shit and piss out of the carpet."

For the second time, she caught everybody off guard. I was flabbergasted. After I gained my composure, I thought her boyfriend probably told her to go to the store and get something to take the "shit and piss" out of the carpet. Being a foreigner, she probably took him literally and stated what he wanted verbatim.

For any of my readers who have pets and, therefore, urine problems in the carpet, this could be educational for you, too. I explained to her that surface deodorants did not work to get the odor out because the problem was inside at the bottom of the carpet. Yes, I could give her something to remove the surface stains, but to do the job right, she would have to inject an enzyme directly into the affected area with a hypodermic needle. (We sold animal hypodermic needles and they worked well.) I explained that the enzymes worked by absorbing and digesting the problem. I told her, for the best results, to use overkill when injecting the enzyme to make sure the area was saturated. I didn't get into using the black light procedure. I thought she had enough to remember, and I did not sell the black light anyway.

Actually, it's usually referred to as the black light box (UV-A), and for those who are interested, it's available on Amazon.com. It works by highlighting the problem area while all normal lighting is turned off.

"You Are the Toughest Lady Executive Housekeeper That I Have Ever Called On!"

I had nothing to lose because I knew there was no sale here

I saw the look on her face as she came down the stairs. I read it as "I'll get rid of this salesman, quick."

Sure enough, that's exactly was she proceeded to do. Everything was "no." She was just determined to get rid of me as quickly as possible.

That's when I just said what was on my mind: "You are the toughest lady executive housekeeper that I have ever called on." And it was the truth! I saw a smile creep across her face. She didn't take it as an insult; she took it as a compliment. Being a woman, she may have been trying to prove herself and justify her position. In her mind, that statement I made confirmed her credibility. She continued to open up, and I actually wrote a small order. Again, in my mind, I had nothing to lose. You just never know.

Money Makes the World Go Around

But nothing really happens until a sale is made

As soon as a sale is made, the action starts. The salesman makes a commission, and the manufacturer puts his or her employees to work manufacturing the product. Then the trucking company has a driver deliver the product to the distributor. The distributor has the employees store the stock in the warehouse. The salespeople man the phones. Other employees pack the orders for delivery to the retailer. The retailer has his or her employees put the stock away and stock the store shelves. Then the salespeople come on to the floor to sell the merchandise, and on and on.

My Negative Sales Close Ended Up To Be a Positive

I had a large bowling alley that was a good customer for years, and then the owners sold their business. This is about my experience on my first call after the new owners had taken over.

I figured I had such a good relationship with the head maintenance man, who also did all the purchasing for the bowling alley, that I could reconnect with him to start. Unfortunately, he was gone, too.

I knocked on the office door of the new head man. *He greeted me with, "You salesmen take so much of my time."* Not a very friendly or cordial welcome and, of course, it rubbed me the wrong way. However, being a professional, I did not react in kind.

Instead, I kept my cool and replied, "Sorry about that, but of course, it's the salesman who brings you the news from your industry and introduces new products that can make maintenance of your equipment easier and more efficient. From your greeting, I gather that you have had a few salesmen calling, probably trying to get your business. I do understand where you are coming from, so I will make it as short as possible."

I introduced myself as the supplier for his operation under the old owners. I assumed that the salesmen calling on him had been telling him how great their products were, how competitive they were, and how great their service was, etc. I avoided that type of presentation and ended up with a negative sales approach.

"You know, Mr. Prospect (Jackass), you have quite a responsibility here making sure the equipment and the lanes operate flawlessly. The fact that we have supplied the old owners for years should speak for itself. However, you don't know me or my company or my products, so it surely makes sense to check out the competition. You may like their pricing better or even their products. Maybe they can offer you something I can't. If I don't hear from you, I'll assume you went with another company. If that turns out to be the case, I would like to wish you luck in your new operation, and if I can be of any assistance, just give me a call."

He contacted me a week later to come over and write an order for supplies.

The Start of My Career—
Selling "Babee Tenda"

I started my sales career selling Babee Tenda safety tables after I received my army discharge. This product was a thirty-inch-square, brightly colored, nicely decorated, well-designed safety table. It was set up so the baby would sit in a swinging seat at the center of the table. The idea of the product was its safety.

Every year, there are many injuries and deaths due to babies falling out of high chairs or slipping past the safety strap and choking against the tray or strap. This table could not tip over, so the baby could not fall, nor could he or she slide down and choke. It was on steel legs with castors that could be extended to allow the table to be rolled from room to room. When the child got older, it could be converted into a play table.

With the accessories, it replaced approximately $500 worth of baby furniture. It sold for $250. Note: Our sales leads came from hospitals notifying us with names and addresses of new mothers. Here are two of my most memorable sales with this product.

Babee Tenda Sale #1 — The Hot Button

I remember that they were a handsome couple, and this was their first baby. The unit always made a nice demonstration, and this was no exception. The husband was very enthusiastic about the product and wanted it. He said to his wife, "Honey, we really need this for the baby."

She was more cost conscious and replied, "I don't think we can afford this right now."

I saw the look on the husband's face. He was disappointed, but he had to support his wife. He said to me, "Sorry, I guess we will have to pass." I had one last chance. I tried something that had been effective in past sales calls.

I said, "Mrs. Jones, when you were in the hospital, you always had a nurse nearby to help you with any assistance that you needed. Now that you are at home, you are by yourself. When your husband is at work, it's all up to you. This is where the Babee Tenda is invaluable. It's like having an extra helper on hand. Since it has castors, you can roll it anywhere in the house you go. You don't have to carry the baby everywhere."

I had hit the so-called hot button. All of a sudden, her eyes widened and lit up. In her expression, I could see the wheels turning as she thought about how helpful the Babee Tenda could be to her. I saw it happen; she was sold! I thought, "Okay, I know you're sold; now turn and let your husband know that you want it." The husband was still trying to let me down easy, when his wife said, "You know, honey, I think the Babee Tenda could be beneficial after all, and help me quite a bit with the baby."

I made the sale! What happened here? I hit her hot button—everyone has at least one or more. She saw the advantage of the rolling Babee Tenda, making life with the baby that much easier.

Babee Tenda Sale #2—One of My More Stressful Sales

It was in the afternoon and the woman's husband wasn't home. I presented the Babee Tenda, and she was thrilled with the product. She wanted it but said her husband would have to approve the purchase. I made an appointment to come back and show her husband that evening.

When I returned, the husband caught me off guard. I discovered he was in the service but not in uniform, so I didn't know his rank. Not that it would have made any difference. This guy had a real attitude. His wife seemed afraid of him and obeyed his every word. He didn't talk with her; he ordered her. I thought it might have been an abusive relationship, but I really did not see anything specific. Anyway, I was aware this guy had issues, and I knew to tread softly.

During my demonstration, he challenged almost everything I said. It seemed like because his wife wanted it, he was going to prove to her that this product was not worth buying and she did not need it. So, I took a different tack. Since he was acting the tough guy, I decided to make a strong, direct, somewhat in-your-face demonstration. I started with the oak frame of the table. "This table border is made of hard oak. If you tried to pound a nail into it, the nail would actually bend." I continued on in this vein.

When it came time to demonstrate how strong the metal legs were, I sat down and placed the table upside down on my lap. I then asked him to test the strength by trying to bend the leg. He did not just test it; he literally attempted to bend it as I knew he would. It held and he looked impressed. The coup de grâce came when I righted the table. I didn't just right it, *I actually slammed it down as hard as I could, and he flinched.*

After all that, he must have been impressed. He asked me a couple questions and almost sounded civil. At that point he seemed ready to buy, but no way was he going to show weakness. Instead, trying to portray himself as a great guy, he said to his wife, "Do you want this?" She nodded and, in a half-whimpering voice, said yes. *He said, "Go into the bedroom and get the cash out of the dresser." I thanked them for the purchase and left.*

What we learned here is, depending on who you are dealing with, you may have to modify your presentation accordingly.

We Really Did Close Six Out of Six Sales Calls!

Additional thoughts to consider

That fantastic, remarkable week with my trainee was surreal. He and I actually closed six out of six sales, with just four sales hours each day! The conclusions are now facts. If you find the problems that the potential customer has been living with and you solve them, the chances of a sale are compounded. But what other factors were involved?

This trainee paid me good money for a U.S. Research & Chemical franchise, and now I had to take him out into the field and show him how to make cold calls. If he couldn't make cold calls, success would be difficult to accomplish. Was that a driving motivational force for me? Yes, stressfully motivating, and in a distinctly positive way. I had to prove to my trainee that his money was well-spent.

Were two very profitable sales in a row a motivating factor? Yes! It was a big boost. How about after three sales or four sales in a row? Yes! That was additional confirmation that the sales plan was working, yet, at the same time, we were having a difficult time believing what was happening. It felt like it was just too good to be true. Nevertheless, the momentum was carrying us forward. We simply could not do anything wrong!

I relate this to being "in the groove"—when you are playing golf or tennis, or running a twenty-six-mile marathon, and you are performing flawlessly. When you are in the groove, you end up shooting the best score ever or running your best race ever. We were definitely in the groove (or in the zone). We performed flawlessly.

Do all of these factors enter into our successful week? In my opinion they absolutely do. I am sure most of you readers have had similar experiences.

Although we were fortunate to find problem after problem just by driving through the Palm Desert/Palm Springs area, you may have to go *inside* the mall, hotel, resort, or restaurant to find problem areas. Of course, your own accounts should be the most obvious places to find business that you may have overlooked.

For example, referring back to the green-painted floor with the extreme wax buildup along the edges, I first spotted the problem by going *inside* the restaurant, and by solving it, I was able to take over the account. (What happened to the salesperson who already had the account?) We spotted the wood floor problem after we went *inside* the resort and the alkaline-covered glass problem after we *entered* the bar. Even though I'm retired now, I still find myself automatically looking for problems (which I spot all the time). I guess it's just in my blood.

Could we go out next week and sell another six out of six? Possibly. However, there is no doubt in my mind that this sales technique really works, and I would expect, **if not a 100 percent closing ratio, at the very minimum a 40 percent to 60 percent closing ratio!** Go out there and prove it to yourself!

In all modesty, I'm a top professional salesman and was always in the upper 10 percent of the companies I worked for. Before I went into my own business, I did very well as a sanitary/janitorial supply salesman, and throughout my sales career, I always worked on commission. You almost always come out better on commission. My father-in-law sold restaurant installations, which included grills, stainless steel hoods, and equipment. This was big business and he made good money. So, *what* you are selling is a factor, too.

So what is bothering me? Most salespeople are gone after a couple of years. Why? If they would stick it out, they could make more income than a doctor or an attorney. In the janitorial/sanitary supplies field, I found that the salespeople just didn't last. They seldom studied sales or maintenance books. They would wing it most of the time, which doesn't work, and that's one of the main reasons they were gone so quickly.

Anyone should be able to handle the vacuum sale to the small local airport. That's a given. But remember, that salesman *could not close*. In the convalescent hospital, I got into that account because I was able to help Jose with some window cleaning tips. Could I have gotten into this account without that know-how? Possibly, but I had a natural in.

The terrazzo floor test patch was critical in making that sale. Can the average sanitary supply salesman make that basic test patch? The sale with the wax buildup was a given if the salesperson spotted the problem and followed up on it. The health club with the white residue on the floor needed my particular expertise. The average salesperson probably would need an alternate path and of course that might work, too.

Many salespeople are not at the level that I or any true professional has been able to attain. They would not have been able to *see* the problems, let alone *solve* them, as we did in our six sales.

I'm not trying to be negative here, just pointing out why the average salesperson may have some difficulty doing what we did. **Nevertheless, they can find the** *problems that they feel they can solve and still be very successful. True professionals are educated in all aspects of their chosen field. They are successful because they have the knowledge to do what we did with our sales technique.*

I think that's part of the reason I decided to write this book. My hope is that, with the right information and inspiration, any salesperson can find the incentive to learn what they need to do to stay in the game and find success.

No matter what field you are in, if you truly want to succeed and make a good to great income, you must be committed. Don't just wing it; that never works. Whatever you are selling, know your products inside out and the competition's products, too!

In Closing, Here Are Two Fantastic Books That I Recommend Highly

These books influenced my life greatly.

The first one is **Think and Grow Rich by Napoleon Hill**. His goal was to interview millionaires around the United States to find out their secrets of success. Listening to and following the principles in this book will change your life.

The second book is **The Power of Positive Thinking by Norman Vincent Peale.** This book will change your life, too. I use these principles every day.

If you have any questions, comments or information,

I can be contacted at berngur@aol.com

Thanks, I trust the book was beneficial,

Bernie Gurstein